salmonpoetry

Diverse Voices from Ireland and the World

The Detachable Heart

Poems by

RACHEL COVENTRY

salmonpoetry

Published in 2022 by
Salmon Poetry
Cliffs of Moher, County Clare, Ireland
Website: www.salmonpoetry.com
Email: info@salmonpoetry.com

ISBN 978-1-915022-20-2

Cover & Title Page Image:
Inigo Batterham

Cover Design & Typesetting: *Siobhán Hutson*

Printed in Ireland by Sprint Print

*Salmon Poetry gratefully acknowledges the support of
The Arts Council / An Chomhairle Ealaíon*

for John Coventry

(1940–2020)

Contents

1

2

3

1

The Detachable Heart

What sort of person pulls a bleeding heart
from her breast and holds it up to the light?

One that grew up in a Catholic house
where Christ is often depicted heart out.

If I presumed detachability
well, it is simply a matter of fact

a heart can still pump when the brain goes dark
and a brain can still fire with a stopped heart.

So do not say it's metaphorical
Pretty man, I loved you with an unfastened organ.

Look at this little lesion you caused-
healing nicely now.

I will wear the scar proudly.
It will be my next collection.

Winter Solstice

We are having a conversation about the impossibility of monogamous love. I have had this conversation before. Sometimes it is philosophy sometimes foreplay. In conclusion I say *but sex is an unknown quantity*. He seems suspicious but I'm lying. I have already sketched its dimensions in my mind. He worries I will lose perspective. He thinks I am a river running heedless to the sea to be destroyed

but for cold water coalescing into pools like screaming ghosts. In different times, I have pushed this conversation every which way it can go. It used to end with a window opening onto the longest night. It used to end with the cold. Now the window stays closed. The darkness isn't real, there is nowhere left to go.

I have clothed myself in this conversation. I have worn it loose or tied it up in a ponytail in the same way as I used to wear myself then slip out of myself. The next day, find myself crumpled on the floor and put myself back on. I have straightened myself, applied lipstick without a mirror. I have met this man before but now I have an app that scans what we once referred to as his soul.

Porcelain

Sometimes,
if you grasp
the concept, you
don't need to see
the art. A urinal is
a urinal after all. I
imagine all the faces
in the gallery, looking
at the Fountain; some are
aghast, some are clever and knowing,
some are bored because they have seen the
future. Of course, whoever's seen the future is bored.
Now, it is clear a concept is not enough because-some
faces are clever, some are bored. Despite this, if I could
decide on what concept best fits this poem, I'd save you
the time it takes to read it. Even though everything has
changed since then. Your faces are inscrutable
and the fountain in the Tate is not
even made of porcelain.

Laughing

(after Maggi Hamblin's painting)

No matter what I say
you will never see his laugh
as Maggie Hamblin's lover
throws back her head
in the wild ecstasy
of hilarity, a wave captured
in the instant of explosion.

I cannot show you,
how his laughter
folds him the other way
into himself, a waxing moon
stuttering on water.

I have no paint, only words
and words are so duplicitous,
this very evening, for instance,
that faceless grin teeters on rivers,
oceans, and rain collected
in basins, bowls, and saucers.

Horizontal-Black

(after a 1980 Sean Scully painting)

If I call you it will only satisfy me momentarily and then I will want to call you again so I will not call you. I will call you. You are a perfect man ifestation of an ambivalence, almost like how an atomic bomb is made. I want to tell you to take vitamin D but I do not care if you take it. There is no resolution, just temporary relief. Then it all starts again with another pretext, another call. Nothing assuages this need. It just creates war. Put these two people together so they can fascinate each other. A nuclear bomb for your home, or is just the genesis of a family. I can hold off for four or five days, if I'm strong, then a pretext occurs to me and it seems like reality. I write such pretty poems; poems of longing. Love is a con cept, we accept as self-evident. What have I forgotten? Are you just a man nequin to hang a fantasy on? If it wasn't you, would it be someone else? Nobody has eyes like yours. No one else would do. How I long for you. How I long for me. I find it difficult not to mention you in conversations about normal things; things people are allowed to say. I feel so high as I give myself away. You are such a buzzy pleasure. You are such perfect pain.

Venery

If I could reach out to touch you, across
the stretch of this pitiful landscape,
where our mothers and fathers starved
to death, I would. Afterall, it is only a
synaptic flash, a wet imperative, a signal
pulsing the length of a nerve. I can pick
up this cup easily enough, there is no sin
in that, but alas the same action of
raising an arm towards your cheek is like
to aiming a rifle to kill a beast.

Muse

Now
that I am alone
there are no more
poems. Oh Rachel, get
serious, the muse was only
ever a manifestation of toxic
masculinity: Gauguin's child
bride, Picasso's women,
a harlot lying naked on a
chaise longue. An excuse
to make vulnerable girls
take off their clothes, the
male gaze hardened into
art. Why then for poems
to come must I be in love?
Not, of course, the sort of
love that would make me
into someone's woman;
not the sort of love that
does the school run, but
rather, this crazy parade
of difficult men each held
to the light and examined,
each held to the light then
put down. Love as a game,
like language. Love as way
to speak something, that is
lost the moment it's spoken.
Is there anything left to say?
I do not think so. I am alone
and poemless. Oh Rachel, get
serious, do you not know that
love is a construction and poetry is over?

A Fig

Many years ago in Turkey
I walked among trees
with a man who reached
up and took a fruit.
He offered it to me.
I did not know
what it was.

It was before
they had them
in Sainsbury's.
I didn't even know
that this was a grove.

I had no notion of beauty then.
I had never seen a fig except on TV
or in a reproduction of a Dutch still life
in a glossy art book in someone else's house.
They were always quartered or halved

to present the flesh. I didn't
even know if it was
to be eaten.

First Person Shooter

God, a smooth skinned boy
with golden hair,
alternates easily from first
to third person view,
sometimes taking aim,
sometimes watching Himself kill.

We discuss philosophy and He shoots from the hip
the bullet takes the shortest distance
to my chest, a direct hit,
but it does not pierce the skin.

I tell Him it's all a question of where you begin.
He is unconvinced.
He thinks me silly, sitting here
holding up this tea-stained mug
at this old kitchen table with its bills and lists,

when He is always, already outside of all this.
He thinks he's won, but he should be careful lest
I drag Him down here, with me, into this mess.

A Happy Man

The men of my childhood were unhappy.
They wore suits and smoked cigarettes.

They never cried but one died
frozen on a park bench.

One I visited in a psychiatric hospital
made pictures with nails and thread.

Although my grandfather seemed content
his lungs were black in his chest.

The men of my youth played chess
in a bedroom room, listening to punk.

They planned how to hang themselves,
scratched ciphers into their flesh.

Later on, the men I knew were drunk
or numbed-out in some other way.

One told me he didn't understand love—
but by then it was way too late.

Even Angels Will Fall

(After the 2012 commercial for Lynx antiperspirant)

On the day we finally moved into the e-world
we discovered many could not handle the transition.

We put their virtual bodies into zip file institutions
on the slim possibility that one day we could wake them.

The first weeks were all about the candlelit vigils
but eventually we just got on with it.

Some flourished, especially those who hadn't
had much truck with reality to begin with.

We programmed our own laws of physics.
I became a blond angel modelled on one I'd seen

in an old TV ad for antiperspirant.
I landed on the pavement next to my ex

but he had missed the point entirely
and was still bitter and old and unimpressed.

Privilege

My privilege is why I need only write love poems.
I am alone in my white room.

I would like to leave, but
my privilege was bequeathed to me

by my father
who passed me into the unkind hands

of other white men
broken men, like him

the grandsons of coal miners.
of farmers.

Of course, I know my privilege is ontological
underneath the soil

there are white bones
like my own, stiff and brittle,

spanning the entire world.
I am the background, the page

on which love poems are written and erased.
I know you don't care to hear it

but my father's leaving ripped the soft pink tissue
of my voice, making two serrated blades.

Maybe you can't hear them come together
but I will be cutting nonetheless.

Punctuation

Let's reduce everything to grammar
a simple matter of where one thing
ends
     and becomes another I've
never known how to use a comma
let alone a semi-colon or a full stop
I'd like to punctuate but
                the rules
always struck me
         as haphazard
especially when all these years later
I still feel the absence of my father

Poetry

Your absence had arms, legs,
wavy hair, and lips.

It sat on the sofa looking sorry for itself,
like you did when things were getting intense.

It wasn't generally in the bedroom
or the kitchen, which was amazing,

because that's mostly where we conducted our situation.
Despite this, I became so accustomed to it

loafing around the sitting room
that I piled it high with stacks of unread poetry collections.

When he is already beyond all this
the sheer weight of all that frustrated lyricism.

2

A Cell

My heart, that scrappy little jail
and inside it, you sitting there dejected
growing more yellow and gaunt by the day.
(I saw your thing on Instagram).
I would like to release you, but can't
the doors don't work that way.
If there is a key, I don't have it.

A Nettle Patch is an Impenetrable Barrier to a Child

She doesn't have access to gloves and secateurs.
She doesn't have access to strimmer or saw.
She doesn't have access to weed killer.
She cannot drive earth-moving equipment.
She cannot be trusted with explosives.
They will never let her study architecture.
She cannot enslave men to build a road.
She cannot buy ten thousand tonnes of concrete.
She does not have furnaces to make glass.
She has no will to confine nature to a park.
She does not confuse this place with the map.
Though, in time, she'll find a city black with forgetting
on the High Street, a bar with smokers outside.
He'll tell a joke, she'll flick back her hair and laugh.

A Dawn

For sure we were in the dark
but the city glittered around us,
beyond it, countless others
and above our heads, galaxies
spun inexorably.

All the pinpoint possibilities,
you among them and tap dancing
or winning the lottery, becoming
someone's mother, or welding scrap
metal into huge clockwork monsters
or maybe just dying.

Stars blinking out, out one at a time
obliterated by the onslaught
of morning light. I am wide awake finally,
this little room, a Tuesday in January.

Connemara

You reckon if you took a picture from every angle
at every time of every day of every year,
the mountain would give herself to you
as she is, plainly. I disagree,

eyes on the road, held down by gravity
I consider the mountain only peripherally
I always impose such linearity
the hills are lonely, *if and only if*...

my heart is the imprint of a mountain,
our eyes are the shape of light
there are no fruit trees here,
the denied thing, in plain sight

it is all just vapour and light,
though surely something must hide.
Still, you renounce the mountain.
Let's agree it changes constantly

but what is it essentially? And us?
What are we? How do we go on with this?
How do we cope? You say you'd go mad out here
but we will pass Maam eventually.

Summer Solstice

I want to know you as animals know each other,
by scent. I already know you humanly.
I know what you say, every possible thing.
Light has sloshed everywhere.
All the dark places are gone.

We opened each other up like oysters
and are empty now. What does it matter?
Everyone is pearlescent.
The sea retreated.
Look at this expanse of flat, grey sand.

Did I tell you I'm taming a feral cat?
She lets me stroke her head as she eats.
It's a transaction of sorts; an equinox
between wild fear and domestication.
Come closer, let me pet you.

My New Favourite

Another woman may have blushed
if you looked at her that way.
I simply added you to my collection
of beautiful porcelain ambivalences,

almost enough to keep me from myself. Oh why
do I lie? The gap between me and I is shrinking
all the while, even as my shelves fill with pale figurines.
You are my new favourite, so serious.

A wiser woman would've smiled and looked away
but I built my home on this empty tension, bricks stacked
in running formation, rafters point in opposite ways.
A precarious location for fine-boned china.

My mother used say I was contrary.
Come on, let's break something.

Night Bus

We are up against it now
that the end has become
comprehensible. I remember

when it wasn't. Do you recall
driving over that hill into Mega-City One?
The future is over, like young love.

The question now is how much
will it cost to keep the teeth in my head
till the end? How much will it cost

to keep my teeth in till I'm lowered
to my final resting place in a corner
of Rahoon Cemetery?

Men are like buses. There will always be
another but I haven't really committed to walking
till I've gone too far to run back to the stop.

Once I'm that far gone, I must contend
with the fact it may pass me, its passengers
held together in the light;

its passengers held together in the static
of being randomly assigned to this particular journey
with nothing to do but ignore each other stoically.

Even so, I will be alone out here
out here with the ghosts of wolves
and rapists still in their flesh. I will be jealous.

Once you told me you were beaten up
and how after a while the punches no longer hurt
they just felt like air moving.

You murdered my longing

And because poetry is so close to longing,
it sickened too. Now, in my notebook
I write a recipe for couscous.
I will cook it for you, pick mint
from the garden, let it simply be mint.

Watch you eat, wordless and content,
until I can't help myself but express
the sudden chill of an October evening,
find myself speaking, *Precarious lover,*
is my longing merely sleeping?

Therapy

I peel off explanations
as I would cotton or denim;
jeans, t shirt, bra, pants
layer after layer examined
and discarded, each sufficient,
but incomplete, especially now
they are emptied.
Even my final
nudity is a deceit,
a lie spoken
so frequently
I believe it.
Go on,
he says,
strip.

I Spend Time in the Company of a Woman Who Does Not Like Me

Sometimes, in a half-dream,
I lose my bag, my purse
is always stuffed with fifties
for some real but unknown reason.

Then it dawns on me I am sleeping
and I force myself awake long enough to know
my bag is on the floor. I run from me
to me, back and forth. In between is a version

of everything, the woman who doesn't like me
who looks away when I ask how she is,
whose voice cannot conceal the lie,
as she tells me she is fine. And men too,

there are so many men between me and I.
I tried to evacuate them one at a time
but there was always one, hard-eyed
with bored hunger. How we're condemned

to want each other. How is that fair?
But still I'll say, *oh woman who hates me,*
his skin is cream. I drowned in it
and now I'm sated.

But Knowing that Poems are Things we can Put on Shelves

(After Dorothea Lasky)

Tonight there's six hours
and one minute of darkness
I need to make the best of it
tomorrow it will be less
but on I blaze
relentless.

I decide action will save me
it's the usual story,
if I do Pilates,

declutter
bring my books to Charlie Byrne's
where some girl in the future
will find them think them plausible,
inspiring even.

I do not care about you women
coming after me, making me
a footnote in your theses.

It's too late, I'm burning
and I'm making a pyre for you.
Young woman you will burn
and it won't matter
what you do.

Your love poems aren't true.
If there was a man here now
I'd hate him, in his absence
I hate myself, the dog is downstairs

I hate her, the dawn chorus
is so feeble these days.
Take these birds away.

Leave me with a single magpie.
Let grey light stretch across me.
Let me get on with it.

Abyss

In 1654, the French philosopher Blaise Pascal's coach was almost thrown off the bridge at Neuilly-Sur-Seine. Afterwards, he became convinced that an abyss had formed on his left-hand side.

Every night I sleep alone on the left.
A lover once pushed me to the edge.
When I told him, he laughed and said
we all have our quirks. I've learned
to stop saying it
to friends
I am accustomed to their walking on air.
Unlike Pascal's, mine opens to the right
and unlike him I was only a child.
I do not think there was a bridge
but I do not remember the incident
or how the world felt before it split.

Poem for Amit

I confess I felt very little
until walking back to the university,
with the cold of the rain in it

and nothing to bring me out of myself
no sun gleam, no promise of anything
but so many days just like this one

stretching back and forward to infinity
and if I settle in on this reality,
I understand what you did.

I walk on past the Cathedral's shadow
(where my own parents were married)
along the inevitable axis of my life,
and rain fell for the millionth time.

Optimism

Cigarettes come in packs of
twenty-three now with a picture

of a cancer victim. Oh, to walk
into a shop and say *twenty-three*

John Player Blue please. In difficult
times, we seek out the familiar

but this city is only a facsimile,
a point by point replica;

a Quincentennial Bridge
still spans a river,
                    etcetera.
                              A woman jumps,

a young mother
                (God help us)

Let no one judge her.
The black water pushes on relentless

(but look how beautifully the moon
dances on its surface).

Travail

I dream I am having a relationship
with an unknown man whom I may
or may not recognize from life.

Our attempts at sex are thwarted
by someone continually knocking at the door.
I awake to a text on my phone

Since the divorce, I haven't written a poem.
I send back something kind although
I know it's empty. I understand exactly.

the dream ended with a woman and man
facing each other, like any two people moving
closer and then apart on an airport travelator.

Pretensions

I realize now I needed my mother
to be rooted in something other
than margarine and nylon,
a fabric no longer relevant

though I remember the way it melted.
and what it was like to slice a tomato
in the seventies; my mother sliced them
from the top. I decided to cut them across

from left to right. I made words into threads
that stitched one thing to the next.
Once, I even made a doll, an effigy
of an ex. In the end, I threw him

in the recycling bin, but as I sewed,
I watched the World Cup.
The sound of a thousand men cheering
had a soothing effect, something to do

with my father before he left. I used to pretend
to care about football, but all I wanted
was to drift off on the brine of human voices;
all I wanted was to be carried away.

At some stage, I learned to make ragù properly
Today, I can no longer be bothered.

Facebook April 2020

Look, this butterfly flew into my house
Look, the wild yellowness of gorse
Look at the Easter cake I made
This purple crocus stands by itself
New Yorkers applaud at 7pm
Spanish nurses clapping at a window
for one of their own
Look at this Fabergé egg
Why not lock up the elderly
and let us back to work
Fuck joggers panting right past me
I don't care who unfriends me
Quarantine sucks
Children scream
in a Bristol tower block
I have hit a sort of plateau
These beautiful poppies in Paros
An old lady stands at her door
I've accepted the challenge
Our son died
Vitamin D builds Covid resistance
Look, I made these Irish coffees
Look, the M1 is empty
Look at the moon over DC
Can you look at me?

You Pretend Nothing is Wrong

All those sunshine words
and in their shadow, the other you.

Let's not get into what's true
(You left me to my dereliction.)

but we all live in two houses
no matter what we do.

In the end, all my mother
wanted was to sleep in her own home.

I said *but Mum, this is your house.*
No, she said, *what about the other one?*

We Discuss The End of our Relationship

If love is sustenance,
ours was just honey or cream,

things you didn't like the feel of
on your fingers,

sticky and insubstantial,
a summer holiday without end,

life without toothpaste
or bullies,

but still in two aspects,
as a dress has an outside and an in,

next to the skin, seams blanket-stitched
to prevent them fraying.

Some fabrics are so fine
they are ripped by existing

(your cheek against mine)
I miss its sweetness.

A Warning

Did I ever tell you that
once I loved someone very hard

but almost entirely unbeknownst to myself.
You know how it goes,

I was young, I thought I could decide.
You are young now,

and have yet to discover
love's strange to capacity to hide.

Decades later when he died,
love showed its winning hand

like a magician sawing a woman in half
TA DA!

3

The Heart Healed

Sara responds with a real heart
an anatomically correct emoji
blue and pink and red
complete with coronary artery.
Something brutal and ancient,

the human propensity to dismember
gone only for the last few moments
of our history. John's head, for instance,
a gift to a difficult wife, and it occurs to me
that, finally, I am ready for some piece
of my ex served up on pale crockery.

Arthur's Seat

After my father died, the plane I took to his funeral
descended into Edinburgh. For the first time
in decades the shadow inside me
lined up with the dark hill that cast it.

It was like an epiphany
or how being giddily attracted
to someone, makes everything fit
into place,

though only momentarily,
within minutes of landing, you have
to figure out where you're going,
turn your phone back on.

Supermarket Gladioli

I write poems about sex what else is there now but
this parade of little gods that blaze and are put out
and plastic-wrapped gladioli. I picked the ones
without a single bloom, succulent antlers,
in a vase on the table, standing defiant.

I do not want them to open but they do, in amethyst,
one by one from the bottom, such unbearable softness,
tissues offered to the uncrying, an unexpected kindness,
a love unbidden and unrequited, creeping up
a single vertebra at a time.

The End of The Exile

I left the world of men
incognito, wrapped in my flesh,
my sunglasses, my shawls, in navy
or black, wrapped in my rage.

I went to live in my mother's house,
made a meal three times a day,
morsels for women, delicate things.
I scraped ashes from the grate. Years passed.

When the carers came to tend to my mother
we talked of female concerns;
the foolishness of men. The foolishness of men
is always the same be they Irish, Ghanaian,

or Lithuanian. We laughed
the knowing laugh of women.
When my mother passed away

I was left with the dog, a gentle bitch
but not enough to maintain the femaleness
of this place and quite unexpectedly, I left my exile,
as a swimmer strides back in to the cold bay.

I kissed him deeply, lowering myself in.

Ow

From the front, a word is a thing
from the back, a sound,

a box big enough to cage a vowel.
At five a.m., I wake to a noise inside or out

Sometimes a sound is the same as itself
Sometimes a word is a howl.

Come Home

Oh, I know you won't be taken in
by a primitive animism but I tell you
your city is miserable. It lies heavy
on the horizon, curled around the bay,
like an apathetic teenager under
the sky's white duvet.

                     I know you'll say
it's just my subjectivity displayed and
projected onto Galway, but honestly
I've never seen the city like this,
its people are grumpy, the traffic's
worse than normal. It's not me
missing you, but the city, it's so maudlin.

Time Travel

It was not like in the movies.
No blinding flash or falling
naked into an American alleyway,
with a stunned beggar turning to look,
with astonishment, at his bottle.

It was just the high street at three-
thirty on a Thursday afternoon.
I walked into the greasy spoon
and it became twenty years earlier
and there you were, younger

than I ever remember you being.
Somehow, I knew you were waiting
for the me I'd been, so I took a table
by the window. What else could I do,
but order tea and wait too?

On time as usual, I tied the dog
by his lead to the wrought-iron railing
and smiled at me, the older woman
who smiled back, but I quickly
forgot me and went in to sit with you.

And I could see how nothing else
existed for me then, but us two
and I knew I couldn't change a thing
so I left again with all my wounds
to let you get on with it.

Grass

Philosophy, I tell this year's crop
is about questions; knowing by now
that questions are places we clear
out to live in.
           Unceasingly, I ask
what is love? Take up gardening;
plant viola, cyclamen, pansies.
They do not thrive, but in autumn
my planters fill up with grasses.

I Wake from the Dream of our Love and Remember Myself

To write something is to see
how little has been said; it is to give up ambition,

accept your own littleness.
Much as life is gathered into its shape by death.

I thought I understood my mother's life
but when she died in January,

the snowdrops bloomed in her scant garden.
Hope is inevitable even though it confuses us.

Soon, snowdrops will mark the end of winter
as usual. I am always torn between hope

and the need to understand.
This morning I awoke

and remembered something of myself
I have a shape already. It is just this.

White Noise

Words are just screams shattered into pieces,
rearranged into poems, excuses, theses.

Sometimes two screams smash into a dialogue.
On occasion, I even discussed politics.

But all I ever wanted was to find the tone
to offset this shrillness,

not to cancel it out.
Silence is whiteness; all noise combined.

All I wanted was the tone that would turn this crying
into waves receding on sand, the murmur of distant traffic,

waking up to my mother downstairs clattering.
All I wanted was someone who could refit

these fragments back to their fullness.
All I wanted was shhhhhhhhhhh

An Argument on Messenger

At the Metropolitan Museum of Art
Cupid attempts to hold Mercury back
I stop to watch, struck by Mercury's
impatient distain.

You and I have also gone to war. The love
I had now dragging at my ankles. I shake it off.
A ping heralds the next offensive.
Sometimes love is foolish; war, destined.

A New Fire

In memory, I still feel
the ease with which we connected

much as ash holds the shape of paper,
even, sometimes, the words in negative

but so delicate as to disintegrate
at the tip of the poker. Why would I

want to read it now? After all,
I threw it to the flames.

There will be another fire
once I've cleaned out the grate.

What seemed an aberration turned out
to be the future; your generation,

are so pretty, if only I could believe
in them, but the bones of the old dogs

are still in their back garden graves.
No matter. This future doesn't involve

significant restructuring of existing
architecture, but the fact I'll stay

here in Westside will seem
strangely miraculous and I will

continue to drive from carpark
to carpark. Don't worry

about that.

October

Let's celebrate on Friday,
let's get a take away coffee
and walk the prom, or
if it's raining, walk anyway,
celebrate our respective lovers
or perhaps by then, the knowledge
our hearts are still supple enough
to recover from them,
celebrate our successes
and failures, celebrate the jobs
we have and the ones we did not get
the children we put off then regretted
not having or didn't depending on the day,
the dogs who died and the one who
will sniff along beside us, busy in himself,
the parents who fucked us up entirely,
the siblings who never made sense,
let's celebrate ambitions met and those
slipping away like summer
leaving us here, shivering and alive
in the cold, sweet grip of autumn.

Thursday Afternoon

(for Kevin Higgins)

Through the open skylight window
the gulls were jealous of the poets
for though we squawked and cawed
like birds, our words made
and remade the world.

Without a past or future to tell of
the gulls tried to shout above us
insisting on this now now now now
We, gracious, gave them their moment
but soon resumed our usual comments.

Have you considered replacing that comma,
putting in something a little stronger?
Someone even suggested a semi-colon,
with that, the gulls relented and flew away
while we found the words of another day.

Clematis

My mother loved wild things
like clematis. She had respect
for anything that disregarded perimeters. To hell with the neighbours
and their territorial claims. Maybe that's more me
than her. Oh, you're a brat she'd say
like clematis; an extravagance of blooms. I am my mother's
daughter. I am what she would have been

if it hadn't been for them. You know they would put me in an institution
for saying what you just said, but even then she said it quietly.
No one needs to flower so furiously,
no one needs to love.
In your honour mother, I'll mind the wild things.
I'll feed the feral cat, love the errant boys.
He had a face you could slap, she said that quietly too
l will slap a face for you mother, I will spread like clematis,
taking up more space than I need. I'll take back the space they took from you.

The Way

As death blooms within you
pressing black and purple
against your skin,

I call in to visit
and despite everything
we maintain the family tradition

of saying nothing
How are you doing? I ask
I'm fine, you say.

I get on with the business
of being middle-aged and afraid.
You, with your drifting in and out.

You say, *sure that's the way.*
It is, I say.

On the Death of an Absent Father

It is a very different thing to remember a place
while it still stands,
even as a ramshackle ruin,
than to remember it once it has been torn down.

The long corridor from the toilets
to the dancefloor, where we sat for hours
surreptitiously pouring vodka from the naggins
in our handbags into our glasses,
is gone.

The Warwick Hotel, broken and dilapidated,
invisible for an age as we drove past it, forgetting
how little hope we had as we attempted to launch ourselves
from that dirty carpet, how little hope
as we adorned the pitiful world with laughter.

The Warwick Hotel is gone. It is an empty plot
that someone will force a future on.

Punishment

I consider you as old Tantalus,
still reaching for his fruit.
You raise your arms to loosen

then gather up your hair
and all my stale cleverness
is instantly erased; but if age

has taught me anything it's that
the heart wants what it wants.
While I live, I relent again and again;
let the ferocious heart love.

Acknowledgements

Thank you to the editors of the following publications who have published poems from this collection: *The Rialto, Stand Magazine, The Moth, Southword, Black Bough, Abridged, Crannóg, The Pickled Body, Dreich, Eunoia, Days of Clear Light: a Festschrift in Honour of Jessie Lendennie, The Children of the Nation: An Anthology of Working People's Poetry, Not the Time to be a Silent Poet: Collected Works, The Galway Advertiser, Drawn to the Light, Ink, Sweat & Tears, Boyne Berries, Fevers of the Mind, Pendemic* and *Books Ireland*.

"Time Travel" and "Winter Solstice" were featured on RTE's Lyric FM *Drive Time*.

Some text in "Horizontal Black" is from RTE's The Works Presents Sean Scully (2015).

Thanks to Words Ireland for selecting me for the National Mentoring Programme in 2018.

Thanks to Patrick Chapman, Michael Farry, Aideen Henry, Mary Madec, and Kevin Higgins, who provided invaluable editorial support.

Finally, thanks to the writing community in Galway without whom writing this book would have been a lonely endeavour.

RACHEL COVENTRY is a Galway-based poet and theorist. Her first collection *Afternoon Drinking in the Jolly Butchers* was published in 2018 by Salmon Poetry. Her poems have been published in many journals including *The Rialto*, *The North*, *Stand*, *The Moth*, *The SHop*, *Poetry Ireland Review*, and *Abridged*. She holds a doctorate in philosophy from The University of Galway. Bloomsbury will publish her monograph *Heidegger and Poetry in the Digital Age: New Aesthetics and Technologies* in 2023.

salmonpoetry

Cliffs of Moher, County Clare, Ireland

"Publishing the finest Irish and international literature."
Michael D. Higgins, President of Ireland